A MIXING POT OF
POEMS FOR THOUGHT

A MIXING POT OF POEMS FOR THOUGHT

LAUREN STIKELEATHER

NEW DEGREE PRESS

A MIXING POT OF POEMS FOR THOUGHT

ISBN   978-1-63676-600-3   *Paperback*

          978-1-63676-252-4   *Kindle Ebook*

          978-1-63676-254-8   *Ebook*

For my two grandmothers, Chips and Nana.

Thank you for inspiring me always.

CONTENTS

———

So here's my goal for what comes next,
in all this crazy rhyming text:
I wish for you to find in here
a verse that grants you one less fear,
a word that makes you turn your head,
a line that gets you out of bed,
a poem that makes you truly feel,
a thought that you don't think is real,
a phrase that makes you smile wide,
a stanza you can't set aside,
a rhyme that made you think of me
and why I wrote these words you see
because these words that you will read
are things that I thought you might need
to go about your everyday
in a more insightful type of way.

AUTHOR'S NOTE

—

My Nana always believed in the luck of heads-up pennies, no matter where she found them. She would stop traffic if it meant being able to pick one up and put it in her pocket. Each time she'd find one, she would always say, "Make a wish!"

I grew up believing in this kind of good luck and would always make a wish when I found one, too.

When I was 16, my Nana passed away from ALS. Her death was absolutely devastating for my family. It took time to get through, but what kept us positive were all the wonderful lessons she'd left in her wake, including the good luck of heads-up pennies. To celebrate her life, my Uncle Sandy had the idea to write a children's book based on the lesson of good luck. He sent me an email saying he had this idea for a story and wanted to see if I had any ideas on how to write it, since I'd always loved to write.

I thought it was a great idea and was immediately inspired. In fact, that afternoon I sat down and wrote the entire story, in rhyme. Neither my uncle nor I expected that I would write the story in rhyme. I did not foresee how easily the words would come to me.

It was not until I was completely in the zone at the end of the story that I realized this kind of writing was my true passion. The end of the story talks about the story's main character, Henry, and what he discovers true good luck to be. It went like this:

"Then one day he realized
just what good luck meant:
it meant money is time,
and time that's well spent.
It meant knowing alone
that one heart is enough,
but together two hearts
are tougher than tough.

In rhyme, I went on to describe many variations of luck, and finished by writing:

But most of all it meant enduring
all of life's many twists
to find those who prove to you
that good luck truly exists."

And right there, that was it. I discovered the power of rhyming poetry. I already knew storytelling could be done this way, but here I showed myself that emotions could be conveyed this way too. I was so amazingly proud of the story I had written, and my uncle loved it. In fact, my whole family loved it.

From that day on, I used rhyme as a tool to dive deep into emotions—things I was feeling, things I noticed in other people, things that made me think twice—and unlocked a framework that has helped me process certain events and emotions in a world that is constantly changing.

Now, I'm not too old. In fact, I'm actually quite young, but I'm observant. In just a few years, I've watched love evolve from a kind of old-style romance to new-world dating, where emotion is taboo. I've noticed that nowadays we enjoy chasing people, but once we have them, we don't know how to treat them. No one can get a read on anyone, so more emotional games are being played than ever before. And my generation especially feels the harsh consequences of emotional games every day. We are losing touch with each other because it is easier to distance ourselves. The rapid speed of technology has virtually brought us together in many ways but has physically separated us in others. In-person relationships are constantly strained by the need for screens and online attention, and this creates a disadvantage for many young people looking for real connection.

I have seen and experienced all of these themes and interactions first-hand. However, most people do not take particular notice to them in daily life; they are unspoken truths about the world we live in. So, that's why I wrote this book: to expose the unspoken truths that we see but don't *really* see.

In my opinion, poetry is the gateway to emotions. As I have shared my work over the years, I have learned that poetry can access feelings in a way many people can't express in normal words.

What I've noticed, though, is that most people don't view rhyming as a very "adult" genre of reading. My theory on why they view it this way is because most nursery rhymes and children's books rhyme. As a result, I feel that many people carry this young child-like perspective on rhyming into adulthood almost subconsciously, simply because they don't often see many rhymes outside of this setting. I understand how and why this happens, as I read many rhyming children's books when I was young too. Nonetheless, the reason I wrote this book is to prove that rhyming poetry *can* be mature—it can convey relatable, advanced emotions and topics in just the same way that conventional poetry can.

In some ways, rhyming can bring about even more emotion than conventional poetry, due to the specific words that must go into its construction. For example, very few words rhyme with love, a common theme of my book. Therefore, I have the limited choice of the words: dove, glove, shove, of, and above. Now, when you think about love and what it embodies, very few of those words do it justice. So, in rhyming, I must seek alternate choices with my words if I want to explain and evoke the same emotion as a poet who can use any word pattern. This obstacle makes rhyming significantly more difficult, but all the more exciting; when I find the right rhyme and rhythm to express a topic, it is truly an accomplishment.

In all my time of crafting and writing, I have given a lot of love through my (rhyming) words. And in return, I have received just as much love. I have been told my writing is special, and that someday, I would have to get my thoughts out there in a book because "people need to hear them."

So, I am writing this book to share all the ideas I have created with the hope that these ideas will inspire others. These poems are mainly for young adults, specifically young women, who may be feeling some of the same things I've felt in crafting these poems. Whether my readers are questioning the world, learning the ins and outs of love, or simply feeling heartbroken, I want them to be able to pick up my book on any given day and find a poem they can relate to. This book is not meant to be read like a chapter book, but rather in small sections, based on what my readers are in the mood for.

A Mixing Pot of Poems for Thought is a compilation of life experiences in rhyme. It's about love and time. Forgiving and healing. Humanity and change. Optimism and understanding. It's about knowing that even the most impassive people feel and feel deeply. Even if some of us cannot express it, we are all innately linked by what we feel. Although *A Mixing Pot of Poems for Thought* may have similar themes to other poetry books, the way it expresses these themes is unconventional. It is relatable and rhythmic; you have to think about how you read each word, and as a result, you have to think a little more about what each word means. This kind of word-rhythm is empowering to read both in your head and out loud and will give you a new perspective on poetry as a whole.

To me, rhyming is the most beautiful puzzle I've ever had to solve. There are only so many words in the English language that rhyme and crafting each poem to sound unique takes immense time and thought. However, I believe that through this intricate process of piecing emotions together through rhyme, I have come to understand myself and others in an incredible way.

This book has been a slow-moving dream of mine for the past four years, and I am so excited to finally make it come alive.

PART I:

THE INGREDIENTS

——

CHAPTER 1

DISCOVERING THE SWEET

——

Out of Place

In a world that's made
of souls that're new,
I find I see things
from a strange point of view,
for my body is new
and fits with the rest,
but my soul is so old
I can't quite express
the emotions I feel
towards things that I see,
for some things new souls do
just simply aren't me.

Old souls: we're loyal—
a bit like a kite:
we belong to one person
and fly at high heights
while knowing we're anchored
and won't drift away
despite any wind
that might tear us away.

But new souls have evolved,
to be more like balloons,
not grounded at all
as they float to the moon
with no ties to earth
or the ground that they left—

they travel alone
at a speed that is deft.

It's peculiar, this difference,
but so very true—
it's contrasts like this
that divide old and new.

Take the question of love:
does it really exist?

New souls would say no
then give you a list:
-Why love doesn't work
-Why love is unsound
-How love's just a word,
not something that's found.

But I quite disagree
with what they might think,
for in terms of our love,
I believe there's a link
between all the souls
who trust in the old—
on new and improved
they're not always sold—
for discounting what brings
such magic to all
makes me think that new souls
live in worlds far too small.

The tragic thing is
new souls are the norm.
The world as a whole
is shrunk to their form—
many modernized minds
that see only skin deep,
who don't express feelings,
and won't take a leap
to discover what lies
on the side of the old—
in worlds of the new,
there's less to behold.

So in great isolation
we're all left to stand
'til someone who's new
decides to expand
to a world where most things
aren't simple or brief—
where love becomes real,
and is common belief.

Until this occurs,
I sit amongst few
who see the true flaws
of desiring new,
but souls differ lots
and will be what they'll be,
so I'll sit, staying old,
and I'll wait 'til they see.

Say It

If you have a feeling
that's rising inside
and it's bubbling up
so much it can't hide,
you should say it: yes please,
get it right off your chest—
after this you'll feel better
than you might've guessed,
for the things that we feel
aren't meant to be kept,
they're things to be said
and things we accept—
for we all feel things
so we all understand
how it feels to feel something
that's small yet so grand,
and I think it's important
to say what we feel,
for if we don't admit
when our feelings are real
we cannot proceed
or move on and above,
no, we must tell the truth
to the ones that we love.

Because all feelings lost
to words left unsaid
end up like new books
that grow old and unread;

they sit in the corner
with plenty to say,
but as time moves along
they wither away
with just the mere thought
of what could've been,
so you must keep in mind
if you're trying to win:
give something up,
be it ego or pride—
if you value these things
then you must decide
if your feelings are worth
more than how you are seen,
and if you can stand
living life in-between.

If you choose silence,
you're left in the midst
of all you could have
and all you could miss
'cause if you don't speak,
silence speaks with great sound—
there's no words to be heard
and no thoughts to be found,
and unfortunately
we can't see what's not there,
no matter how closely
or carefully we stare—

my point is just this:
none of us can read minds!

But we all have feelings
that are all of all kinds.

So you may as well say it—
it's worth a fair shot,
don't anticipate failure
just think: well, why not?
'Cause the worst you can do
is to hide it away,
so say it, my dear,
say it anyway.

Words That Aren't There

It's hard to describe
something so good
without adequate words
I can't find but I should,
for in moments like these
I can't speak at all—
I'm left in my silence
as I start to fall
for something unknown
that's foreign to me,
but the way that I'm falling
is utterly free.

These things that I feel
make me smile and glow
in a way I have seen
but have never quite known,
yet I stand here before you
with cheeks flushing red,
and a million thoughts
flying 'round in my head.

My mouth has gone mute,
so my eyes speak for me—
they're speaking of things
I can't touch or see—
things that lie just beneath
the thin layer of skin

in which all I feel
is held hostage within.

Your eyes speak the same—
they reciprocate mine,
in a way that sends shivers
the length of my spine.

Together, we stare
in a soft, gentle haze—
seconds slow 'til they freeze
and time simply delays.

We're everything quiet
in a world full of sound
and it's hard to believe
in this moment I've found
someone simple and calm
who is willing to share
a few moments with me
with the words that aren't there.

Eyes Closed

Once a friend asked me why
we kiss with eyes closed,
and I looked at him funny
because really, who knows?

I mean, kissing just happens,
it's a thing that we do,
and it's something quite special
when it happens to you.

But a kiss is a kiss
'til a kiss is a spark
that turns into a flame
that makes light in the dark,
and it's kisses like those
that take you off your feet—
they're gentle and calm
yet arrive with some heat,
for when two lonely people
come together like this
it's a magical thing—
a moment of bliss,
for a kiss has the power
of infinite words
and in kissing someone
all your thoughts can be heard,
which leads me to why
we kiss with eyes closed:

a good kiss is felt
from your head to your toes.

So you don't need your eyes
to be looking for you,
cause you know where you are
and you know what to do,
and you're there with someone
who's wanting the same—
who's chosen to kiss you
from spark into flame—
so instead you just feel
with no need to feel seen;
if you've ever felt this,
you'll know what I mean.

Pull

If it's still on your mind
then it's still in your heart,
and there's simply no way
to pull those apart
for they're so intertwined
in the way that they're built
that if one were to go
then the other would tilt.

See, the heart and the mind:
they're two separate parts—
our hearts hold the love
and our minds hold the smarts,
but the funny thing is
that love makes you dumb,
so when you're in love
your mind just goes numb,
yet it's still in your head
and it's keeping its post;
it's just taken up
by the one you love most.

In some ways, I'd say
your heart's the most strong,
though without your mind's smarts
it can lead you quite wrong,
though I've been there, I've felt
my heart pull me one way
while my mind sits and laughs

saying, "Please do not stray,"
but I find myself leaning
always more toward my heart
'cause I feel that without it
I may fall apart,
for although our hearts
can confuse us a lot
they guide us in life
with the feelings they've got
and they open our eyes
to the wonders unseen—
they are what makes us, us
if you know what I mean.

So although hearts and minds
differ much in their tasks,
in the end they both work
in tandem to ask:
"Is this real? Is this love?
Is this something that's right?
'Cause if you answer yes,
we'll be sure to hold tight."

Refreshing

There are things in this world
more refreshing than most:
like a fresh glass of juice
with your warm morning toast,
or a breath of fresh air
on a chilled winter day,
or a sky turning blue
from a dimly lit gray,
or the cool minty taste
after brushing your teeth,
or returning to bed
with newly cleaned sheets,
or lying in blankets
fresh out of the dryer,
or sitting and watching
flames dance by the fire,
or a cold lemonade
in the hot summer heat,
or a freshly baked cookie
you can't help but eat,
or a jump in the ocean
after naps on the beach,
or the first juicy bite
of a ripe summer peach,
or a drive Sunday morning
through your small sleepy town
with some light music playing
and the windows rolled down,
or the first peep of sun

rising on a new day,
or the first blooming flower
in the middle of May.

There are millions of these
if you just look around—
many sit in plain sight
and are easily found,
but as I'm here thinking
of things of this kind,
I'm realizing one
always comes to my mind:
it's something I love
and am thankful for too,
for I've never known something
as refreshing as you.

Good Luck Charm

In this world, I believe
there's lots of good luck
that exists in the world all the time
and I think that I got
a good bunch of this luck
on the day I could call you all mine.

As years passed me by,
I'd been wishing on things,
always praying for someone like you;
I put faith in life's magic
and chanced all my hopes
on luck not yet proved to be true.

In my walks every day,
I'd look down by my shoes
for a penny heads-up on the street;
I'd smile each time
and I'd wish as I went
on these coins I'd find next to my feet.

I'd look at the clock
when it'd just passed eleven—
sometimes I would catch it just right,
but 11:11
looked the same every time,
and I'd make the same wish every night.

I'd put my hands up
in the brisk autumn winds
and I'd hop, skip, and dance all around,
with the hopes I could grab
just one crisp good luck leaf
before all the leaves hit the ground.

I'd go to my window
on clear starry nights
and I'd sit, watching close for a star
to shoot through the sky
with good luck in its wake,
going so fast and who knows how far.

And for all the eye lashes
I caught on my finger
I'd carefully blow them away
hoping somehow they'd reach
where the wishes are granted;
each time I had faith that they may.

Somehow all this wishing
on small little things
brought me into your sweet and safe arms,
and I strongly believe
in good luck in this world,
for I now have my own good luck charm.

Home

I've often wondered how you know
when you've found the one that's right—
what does it feel like when you do?
I've heard it's something you can't fight.

They say your soul mate makes you calm,
a comfort you have never known,
but of the things that love should feel like,
I think love should feel like home.

It should always seem familiar,
like you're walking through the door
of somewhere you know very well,
where you've been many times before;
a place where you can be serene
without a pounding, racing heart—
a place where you are never anxious,
and where you're a vital part.

Here you should always feel protected—
below the roof, between the walls;
it should be somewhere that you love
to simply wander through the halls—
somewhere that you have come to know
just like the back of your own hand—
somewhere you are met with warmth
and where you finally can expand
to make a love into a life—
to make a house into a home,

to find somewhere to settle down
so you no longer have to roam.

'Cause home's a feeling, not a place—
it has no address, no front door;
it's something built up over time
and starts with someone you adore.

It's your safe haven when you need;
it's your anchor when you drift—
it moves with you as you go
and as your life begins to shift.

It's permanent, this kind of home,
just as the best of love should be—
something you know will never leave,
someone you know will always see
that through your windows and your walls
you're unimaginably rare—
someone who cares for you so much
that they'll be your home anywhere.

This Quote

There's this quote that I've heard,
that you've likely heard too—
it's a phrase that I've learned
is undoubtedly true:

If you care for someone
and want them to stay
you should let them go free—
let them go far away—
for if they return
and come back to you,
they will always be yours
despite all you may do,
but if not, let them go—
let them keep running on,
for they weren't meant to be,
so it's better they're gone.

But the part of this quote
I think no one has said
is a part I made up
before going to bed:

If two people care
and they both care a lot
and they both choose to go
whether they like it or not,
and they get to go forth
leading two separate lives,

and they get to see new things
as new things arrive—
and they *still* both come back
and *still* turn around
and *still* choose to smile
despite any frowns—
well though things like this
can be tough to attain,
they're the strongest of loves
that are meant to remain.

So if you ever find
you're lucky enough
to have someone come back
despite all that's tough,
please don't let them go,
'cause they've shown they are there
for the long haul this time
and won't go anywhere,
for they've realized that life
isn't right without you—
this is something that's precious
but happens to few
so don't take it for granted
or push it away;
this is something that fate
worked to put on its way.

The Stages of Loving

I've noticed with time
that there's levels of love,
some are medium, low,
some are high and above—
these levels, they're tough
to discern in between,
for it's hard to know how
to foresee what they mean.

So we'll start at the base:
liking someone, well yes,
but the bottom is liking
the way that they dress,
and the way that they walk
and the way that they look:
here it's physical traits
that have made you feel hooked,
'cause they look just the part
that you thought you might want,
so they simply stand by
as someone you flaunt,
but you're not really sure
if you'll keep them right here,
or if you're just taken
by the way they appear.

The next level up
is to like them for them,
for it's from this point on

that real feelings can stem,
'cause you've gotten to know them
and all that they've got,
yet you question all actions
and each little thought
that you have about them
because you are not sure
if this feeling will fade
or will stay and endure,
so you like them a bit
and with each day it grows
until something else changes
or something new shows.

The third level up
is to love them I guess;
it's a fairly big leap
from all of the rest,
'cause though you feel things
that are out of control,
you realize this person
makes part of you whole,
and you feel in your heart
they fit in somewhere here,
amongst you and your thoughts
and they start to appear
in your daydreams of things
that you dream will soon be,
and you smile because
when you're with them you see
yourself coming alive
in a way that is strong,

and it's naïve to say,
but you feel you belong.

The big, final step
that takes longest to find,
made of friendship and loving
and magic combined,
is to be in love—
"in," 'cause you're in it, you see,
you're exactly and perfectly
where you should be,
for you've found yourself in
something so very grand
that is built like a beach
with each granule of sand—
from the smallest of things
it has grown into you,
with a heart that is full
and one soul made from two.

These here are the steps
from beginning to end
of the love you can find
and that you can extend
as your life rushes on
and you struggle to see
if you've found someone worthy
of steps one through three—

though I hope at one point
you find just one worth more,

so that you learn the magic
of step number four.

One and the Same

We're all one and the same,
but all one-of-a-kind—
we're the same in the way
that we all want to find
someone fit just for us
who's willing to see
that we simply aren't perfect
but chooses to be
there for imperfect times
when life isn't great—
when we're bogged down with life
and its burdens and hate—
yet who knows that the times
when our smile is full
outweigh the bad days
that may take their toll.

We're all one and the same
but all one-of-a-kind—
we're different in how
all our minds are designed,
for we love different things
yet we have the same doubts—
"How could anyone love me
and all I'm about?"
And we go about life
in a million ways
yet are somehow united
by this doubt that stays

in our heads as we go
wishing someone else knew—
you'd be baffled to know
that it isn't just you.

We're all one and the same
but all one-of-a-kind,
'cause we lead different lives
but we all feel confined
by desires unmet
and by hearts that were broke;
by things we should've done
and words we should've spoke,
for with love comes regret
some that's strong, some that's weak,
some that gives us a voice
or forbids us to speak,
but we grow from this hurt—
to pain we grow blind,
as we slowly turn into
our one-of-a-kind.

This transition is big—
it's a coming-of-age;
it's the you that you were
breaking out of its cage;
it occurs when you see
you can live with more ease
as you start to mature
and start to unfreeze
from the thoughts that held you
in their hands for too long,

and you finally realize
that those thoughts—
they were wrong.

You realize you want
someone fit just for you
who's willing to see
all the good that you do
and who's fully themselves
whether you're there or not,
but who knows that without you
they're missing a lot—

someone who understands
why you doubt what you do;
someone who understands
the things that make you, you.

Because you know yourself—
independent you've stood
for your whole life 'til now—
you deserve someone GOOD:
someone one-of-a-kind
from their soul to their name,
yet to whom that you feel
you are one and the same.

CHAPTER 2

TASTING THE SALT

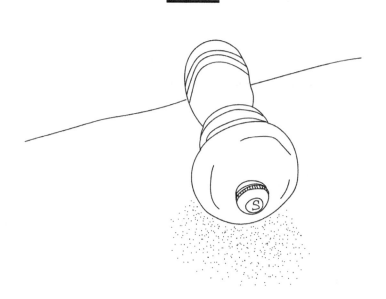

Roots

Losing both your first love
and best friend all in one
is something I've sadly
and painfully done.

It was dreadful and shocking
and hard to move past—
for between us we had
many memories amassed.

There was tension-filled friendship
that changed for the best
when our deep, pent-up feelings
were finally expressed.

There was holding of hands,
and a pact that was made—
a promise of friendship
that would never be swayed.

There was head over heels,
there was head in the clouds;
we saw only each other
as we walked through big crowds.

There were high heels and suits
there was bliss as we danced:
two best friends finding love
feeling oh so entranced.

There was joking about
why it took us so long
to come clean of our feelings
and admit they were strong,
but we trusted ourselves
and we trusted this fate;
we had built something to which
no one could relate,
for at ages so young
no one thought we could feel
in a way that would last:
in a way that was real.

But to this day I know
that when two friends collide
it's a force that is stronger
than oceans or tides;
it's a manifestation
of two loves of two kinds
that are mixed and absorbed
into two separate minds.

So we stayed as best friends
being best lovers too;
I still can't to this day
explain my love for you.
It was something intangible—
a sweet type of high—
that was built from strong roots
that were not meant to die;

they were meant to survive
not be plagued by deceit
by my best friend who made
the decision to cheat.

So when you took a shovel
and dug up our roots
and robbed them of life
and their will to grow fruits,
well I tell you, it crushed me.

I broke in my soul.

For I watched my best friend
dig away at a hole
where our friendship was built
but now ceased to exist
all because of low actions
you seemed to dismiss
without thoughts of how deep
my roots ran for you—
what a sad, careless thing
for somebody to do.

My Two Biggest Fears

I have two biggest fears—
they're not darkness or snakes—
these two fears that I have
are of much higher stakes;
the first fear that I have
is not making you pay,
but the second is throwing
our friendship away.

If I gave you friendship
and let the rest go
then we would be friends
with a lot to re-grow,
but you'd get your wish
and I'd pay the cost,
and all "making you pay"
would be totally lost.

And I want to be friends—
I want nothing more,
for the friendship we had
was strong and we swore
that through what we were
and what we came to be
we'd stay friends 'til the end,
me and you, you and me.

But if you'd given me
a great big crystal ball

at the time of this promise
and let me see it all,
I don't know that my words
would be written in stone,
for back then your true colors
had not yet been shown.

So as I sit here now
looking at the whole you
I find that I'm puzzling
over just what to do
'cause the large sums of hurt
that you brought upon me
don't deserve anything:
not a smile, not a plea,
not a glimmer of hope,
not a sliver of thought,
not the slightest of good,
not a second-time shot,
not a word, not a sound,
not face-to-face talk,
not a laugh, not a chat,
not a clear-your-head walk.

No, you deserve nothing,
but as I wrote that,
I know I'd do it all
at the drop of a hat
for while this seems easy—
this throwing-it-out—
it makes me re-think
what all this is about:

it's about me deciding
and taking the lead—
so I think back to when
both of us, we agreed
that through better or worse
we'd stay strong and stay us
and this saying held something
much stronger than trust:

It held you.
It held me.
It held us as friends.
It held all of life's twists,
all its turns, burns, and bends.

So if you're asking me
what I need from you
to go back to our promise
and see it all through,
I'll tell you one thing,
and I'll say it one time,
and to make sure it's clear,
I won't say it in rhyme:

You need to show me
you regret what you did;
and I need to believe you.

What I Hope For You

I hope one day you find someone
who loves you just like me,
'cause if you do, she'll be a keeper,
and what a couple you will be.

I hope one day you find this girl
and that she's perfect like the sun;
I hope she strips you of your worries
and makes you feel like life's begun.

I hope one day you seek her out
and hold her hand so very tight;
I hope you make her feel so loved—
I hope you always kiss goodnight.

I hope one day you tell her how you feel—
I hope one day she feels the same;
I hope you never hurt her feelings
and never treat her like a game.

I hope one day you cook her dinner—
I hope one day she loves it all;
I hope you two can sit for hours
and talk of topics big and small.

I hope one day she makes you laugh;
I hope one day she makes you cry;
I hope you know her worst but see her best—
I hope she boosts you high.

I hope one day you talk her ear off
about the things you have in mind;
I hope she tells you to go chase your dreams
and to never feel confined.

I hope one day you two can dance
to your own very favorite song;
I hope you complement each other—
when one is weak, the other's strong.

I hope one day that you will know
just how much power love can hold;
I hope it seizes you with force—
I hope you have it 'til you're old.

I hope one day I really mean these things
and not wish *she* was really *me;*
I hope one day that we still talk,
but I hope one day I'll be free.

I just hope one day I will know
that there was nothing I could do
for I have learned you cannot love a person
into loving you.

Without A Trace

Each time I had you in my hands
you slipped like a bar of soap;
I couldn't catch you as you went
but every time you left me hope
that you'd come back to me again
because 'til now, you always did;
you were the one I loved to hate
because with you I was amid
a whirling wind, a perfect storm,
a force of nature I had made—
I liked you more than I admitted
and was nothing but afraid
to lose the parts of you I had
because I only had a few—
these were the parts that roped me in,
so I kept on chasing you.

This is where you really got me,
'cause you loved to watch me run—
sometimes you would let me catch you
just so I could think I won,
and I'd always think I had you,
but you never could sit still—
you fooled me every single time;
I was suspended in the thrill.

The things I felt when chasing you
were unlike anything I've felt;
it was like turning into chocolate

that under heat begins to melt—
begins to lose what keeps it solid,
starts to lose its very shape—
but once I started melting under you
I couldn't find escape.

And it exhausted me—it drained me,
though I still charged on ahead;
with every step in your direction
I let you pull me like a thread—
so I ungracefully unraveled;
over time I came unwound,
except I couldn't help myself
each time you came back around.

You were the one I always ran to—
pure excitement at fast pace;
you were an always-moving target
with a handsome, charming face.

You kept me guessing and I wondered
if I ever made you feel,
except the only problem was
you never wanted me for real.

So you had me in your hands,
but you slipped right out of mine—
this was what you'd always planned for:
this was fully your design.

I was stupid not to see it;
I was blinded by the chase,

but I hope that you don't mind now
as I leave without a trace.

Broken

With you I saw you.
I saw through your act.
You're big and you're strong,
but I know for a fact
that you're broken inside
and less tough than you show:
this is something you never
want anyone to know.

Yet with me you were comfy.
You let me see through,
and I saw you just like that:
I saw you for you.
But the second you realized
just what you'd revealed
and thought that just maybe
this time you might feel
slightly closer to someone
who's patient and kind,
who listens real close
and who's got a bright mind;
someone who's got a smile
that makes you grin too,
someone who makes you question
the you that you knew—

you ran far away
'til you couldn't look back,
for as you ran you burned

every step of your path;
you ran far from someone
that had promise to last
and ignited your feelings
until they were ash.

It was me. I was there.
I stood still and attached
as you crumpled me up
and you tossed me like trash
to the garbage of things
that made you so afraid
you couldn't bear them,
for they pressed and weighed
on your ego, your manhood:
the "you" that you "are"
to the rest of the world
looking in from afar.

Oh you coward, how dare you,
you weak, little man.
Taking shreds of your pride
running fast as you can
far away from all things
far too real for poor you,
leaving me all alone
with no one to run to.

I am frankly quite shocked.
What you did isn't fair.
I'm appalled at how little
that you seemed to care.

But the thing about me
is that I will bounce back,
and to do so I won't need
any form of payback
'cause the power of this—
of this being alone—
is that I can now plunge
into life's large unknown
all while knowing one thing
to be utterly true:
you will always need me
long before I need you.

A Narcissist's Fear

When you leave someone toxic
and things come to end
and you no longer have
all their flaws to defend
'cause you've just gotten rid
of the source of your stress
and for once you can stop
and correctly assess
why you stayed for so long
in that troublesome place;
why you didn't see sooner
that you needed space
from the person who thought
you were just second-best,
and that in their grand life
you were only a guest—

You will question yourself:
"Well, what took you so long?
There was so little right
and so much that was wrong."

But you'll see that it wasn't
your fault, not a bit—
you just wanted something
to which you could commit,
but you'd chosen someone
who lived in a world
that twisted and echoed

and circled and swirled
around only themselves,
never once around you;
despite all that you gave
you could never break through
the thick bubble they had
wrapped around their own head—
one that fooled you so well
and that you had misread
to believe they liked you
as you were and whatnot,
when it really was just
your attention they sought.

You were there for a job:
to boost them up more—
quite a one-sided task
that seems more like a chore,
but you stayed 'cause you thought
you were vital to them
like a flower supported
by the strength of its stem,
when in fact you were not;
you were used as a tool—
someone praising and kind
who just served as more fuel
to the image they had
of themselves in their world
that was so very fragile
that it could unfurl
at the sight of someone
up and leaving their side—

at the pure, honest shock
of just… being denied.

So look back knowing well
that you made the right choice:
you left someone who never
would value your voice
unless you just told them
what they wanted to hear—
losing someone like you
is a narcissist's fear.

Easy

Someone once told me
that all love is fleeting;
it's easier lost than maintained,
for it's simple to lose
when you don't stop to think
about all the things you could gain.

But the issue today
is that no one has time
so nothing is given a chance,
and the hope that we have
for the small things to change
is just lost in the past of romance.

I'm not sure what occurred
or when all this was lost—
when the present turned into the past—
I just think people realized
that effort takes time
in a world that's moving too fast.

But the common mistake
of most people these days
is we run when our feelings get strong,
for we've felt it before
but it scares us so much
that we only think, "What can go wrong?"

We're scared of ourselves:
often far too afraid—
and of this, we're all in denial;
but this fear has erased
what once made romance real,
so now most of it's gone out of style.

It's a thing of the past
to most young people now,
and I fear its extinction will come
when the next generation
forgets how to love,
instead choosing to flee and succumb
to the easier life—
one that's tempted away
many people who tried to hold out
but caved and decided
that love that takes work
is a thing they could get on without.

So convenience has won
and our fears have prevailed;
love is fleeting in front our eyes
like the snow when it melts
or the sand at low tide
or the sun sinking out of the sky.

We're watching this happen
as though we can't change
the direction to which we have turned,
but this apathy towards

things that take extra work
should have everyone very concerned.

Never Really Yours

You say you don't care—
that this thing's just a fling
but when you must leave,
you can't help but cling,
for though you knew well
it was casual and chill,
you realize too late
that you have feelings still.

So you mess it all up
'cause your feelings are more
than the fling that you had
and the ease of before,
'cause it's always too easy
committing halfway,
and sometimes you see
you would rather just stay.

But the thing with these flings
is that one person feels,
then the other one sees
but then loses appeal,
'cause for some, flings are flings;
not the slightest bit more—
they are quite uncommitted,
and like to explore;
they keep options open
to see what they get,

and then leave soon after
with little regret.

In our world this is normal—
"hookup culture" it's called;
it shrinks our self-worth
but we've jointly installed
all its rules in our minds
to resist getting hurt
'cause its whole central purpose
is so we can flirt
and live out our lives
in a way that feels free
from emotions that turn
"me and you" to a "we."

But there's folks who will wait
on a single reply,
one they know they won't get,
'cause they thought they might try
to defy the whole culture
and speak from the heart—
quite a hazardous move
that could tear things apart.

I give these folks credit
for risking it all,
despite the known fact
of what occurs when you fall.

And it isn't their fault
when some people just leave,

but the ones who take off—
they don't have to grieve
the loss of a person
that they understood,
who they'd love to keep seeing,
if only they could.

It's unfortunate, this hurt,
'cause it comes with few cures,
for how do you get over someone
who was never really yours?

The Other Shoe

Am I the only one on earth
who often finds myself like this:
feeling that fear when things begin—
right after having that first kiss?

Yes, it's times like this I find
that I'm putting up a wall—
something of strength to hold me up
in case I do begin to fall.

You see for me, as I have learned,
to fall is utter suicide
because despite my many efforts
I am always set aside
for reasons I don't understand—
things always seem to be my fault;
I'll think I've finally got it good
but then it slowly comes to halt.

This cycle drains me to my core
but every time I know the drill,
and so I need to put up walls
or else I know that I will fill
with feelings that will weigh me down—
the ones I'm not supposed to feel,
the ones that open up my heart
and make it easiest to steal;

I've had parts stolen more than once—
my fragile heart's been chipped away
by thieves who only come for gold
and leave as soon as they get paid.

So here I am, we've just first-kissed,
and I am panicking, you see,
because it's people just like you
who really scare people like me,
because your smile's full of promise
and you don't seem like you're a thief,
but I must keep my walls intact
because of my ingrained beliefs
that no one's good until they prove it—
and no one's worth it 'til they stay
for long enough that I can know
that they won't try to run away.

So if you choose to stick around,
just know I'll hold my walls up strong
until you prove to me you're different—
until you prove to me I'm wrong.

I have faith in you, I do,
I wish my worrying would stop—
but part of me is simply waiting
for the other shoe to drop.

Blue Eyes

I stared in your eyes:
they were pretty, sky blue,
but I saw you were very unsure
of what you should say
or what you should feel—
the blue in your eyes was so pure.

With sadness, you searched
through my eyes to my soul
where my deepest of feelings were hid,
though I'm realizing now
that exposing these feelings
was the worst thing I ever did,
for you took a long look,
then you listened to me
as I told you how much that I cared;
you saw where this came from—
deep down inside—
you took it all in as you stared.

But that blue in your eyes,
it had depths to it too—
it was swirling with storms soon to come,
and I studied it closely
as time inched along
to see where it kept coming from.

Then I saw it right there.
Your eyes sagged a bit;

you were hopeless in finding your words,
but I heard you so loud
that my ears almost cracked
and my very own vision: it blurred.

You'd made up your mind:
you weren't ready for this,
despite all of my kindness and love;
in that moment of truth—
in that moment of choice—
in your eyes, I just wasn't enough.

So with blue in your gaze
and a hand holding mine,
you knew then what we had to do now,
but I saw the tides change
behind all that blue
and it made me just think about... how?

For you knew I was good—
you said so yourself:
I'm unique and deserve all the best,
yet you still let me go
out the door with the wind
like smoke leaving its cigarette.

So I got in my car,
left you standing right there
right after we'd chosen to break;
as I drove I was sad,
but was hit with a feeling:
I finally felt wide awake.

You had opened my eyes
to what I needed most:
to see colors for once that weren't blue,
so I now live in color
with wide open eyes;
this I wouldn't have done without you.

Lost to The Future

To wage war on time
is a war to be lost—
one I don't think we ever will win,
because time is a force
and we're weak in its arms
even if we feel stronger within;
but when coupled with love,
time's distorted a bit;
it's an enemy shrewdly disguised
as your friend for a minute
who then shows its face,
leaving many upset and surprised.

It's sad but so common
when timing is wrong,
we all wonder, *what if it was right?*
and there's many of us
who will battle with it,
losing steam as we push through this fight,
'cause we think that we're safe—
bulletproof with our love,
claiming it can endure time's true test,
when in truth most cannot
despite many attempts
that we make in our avid protest.

But there's me and there's you:
two souls so much alike
fused by passion and laughter and care

sadly fooled by illusions
created by time—
circumstances that simply weren't fair.

You were six whole years older
than I, who was still
beginning to forge my own way;
I was still in the depths
of creating myself;
this was something I couldn't delay.

You were so far ahead,
I was so far behind
that catching up wasn't a choice,
so I stood far behind
as you faded away
'til you no longer could hear my voice.
'Cause you wanted the things
that I just couldn't give
despite all the good that we were,
and the saddest part was:
we were lost to the days
that still had yet to occur.

We were lost to the future
both near and too far,
different paths running two different ways,
and though I'll push on,
I'll hold in my heart
a resentment for timing,
always.

A Short Goodbye

Here we've reached a sure point
where we're done and we're through
not because of one thing
done by me or by you
but because life is life
and we need to move on—
'cause we need to see things
before chances are gone.

I'm younger than you
and you're older than me,
and our lives at this point
are divergent, you see,
for you're settled in life
in a way that I'm not—
I'm someone who still
needs to see quite a lot
and I'm sure with your age
just a few years ahead
you still want to see lots,
from the things that you've said,
but the things that we want
are not one in the same
at this one point in time,
which is something to blame
on the timing of life
not on us as two souls,
for not every two people
can have the same goals.

Though I'm sure at a point
in the future we'd be
in a much better place
to stay close and agree
that we're better together
not better apart—
but right here and right now
I must follow my heart.

I must push on ahead
to the things I must do,
even if that does mean
me departing from you,
and this pains me a lot—
more than you understand—
because you changed my life
more than I had once planned
'cause you showed me one thing
that I needed to see:
that I'm beautiful simply
because I am me.

So I'll say bye for now
with a tear in my eye
that I'll hide very well
'cause I don't want to cry,
but I might because you
gave me hope in a way
that required no time
yet allows me to say
that our time was short-lived
but had magic within—

I have faith if fate's true
I will see you again.

CHAPTER 3

ADDING THE SPICE

—

You Don't Know

You don't know what you have
until it is lost—
and you sit and you cry at the thought
that the person you had
isn't yours anymore—
you know that you've lost your one shot.

It's these moments of grief
when you wish that you knew
just how great what you had really was,
for when life hits you hard
and you make the wrong choice,
you must know you can't simply hit pause.

Good things come and go,
but when you've got it good
you should not be desiring more,
for when you have greed
and you climb up too high,
you risk losing it all to explore.

And exploring is good—
it's vital, in fact;
you must seek out new things as you go,
but before you go out
you must truly assess
what you're sure of and what you don't know.

Once you've made up your mind,
and made your own choice,
I hope it will make you real proud,
'cause when you let things go
without saying just why,
words mean nothing and actions speak loud.

And I do guarantee
when you know that you've lost
this person that's out of your hands,
you'll be brimming with sorrow
and many regrets,
and then you just might understand
how it feels to be broken
to pieces for someone
who keeps going on without care;
when you feel this at first
you'll know what you've done—
you'll be painfully more than aware.

You'll be reckless and angry
but all at yourself
as your person begins to restart
a life that is happy
and full of good things,
in which you don't play any part.

The ones that you hurt
deserve better than you,
and giving them up is what's best,
and all efforts you put

into bringing them back
must be halted and put down to rest.

So to anyone suffering
from the hurt that they've caused
know that this is a pain that endures,
for you let someone go
that loved you for you—
now this someone will never be yours.

One Day

One day I won't be missing you
and you'll no longer be in sight;
one day I'll take a step and won't look back
and finally feel all right.

One day I know I'll close the chapter
and I'll triumph over tears;
one day I'll smile at what's happened—
even if it takes me years.

One day I'll realize that my standards
had been set a bit too low,
and you'll be someone I once knew,
not somebody that I know.

One day my mind will stop the playbacks
and my memories will fade,
and I'll celebrate good times
with the ones I've loved who stayed.

One day you'll simply be a story—
and I'll go and read it through,
and when I one day tell this story
I'll be someone who's brand new.

One day I'll be loved as I love
and I'll get what I have earned,
and I won't fear every day
because one day, tides will have turned.

One day you'll realize what you lost—
you will wake up all alone,
and you may begin to cry
at just how far apart we've grown.

One day someone will bring me up,
but then you'll cringe and say, "Please don't,"
and though you say that you'll forget me,
over time you know you won't.

One day you'll realize what you did—
your memory will bring it back;
and you will see with perfect eyes
the moment where you fell off track.

One day my words will finally reach you,
and you'll clearly hear them out;
you might have hope that I'll return,
except tomorrow you'll have doubt.

One day you'll realize why I stayed away;
you'll feel a broken heart—
you'll feel the same way I did once,
but like me, you will then restart.

One day you'll treasure someone else
and learn that love can truly last,
but there won't be a single day
where you can go and change the past.

The Stages of Healing

Sure it matters right now—
just a moment ago
your love was going
where you thought it'd go,
but the rug was pulled out
right from under your feet;
what a frustrating fate
that you now have to meet,
and I know that this hurts—
you are right to be mad…
but just take a deep breath
and calm down just a tad.

Will it matter an hour
from where you are now?
When you've processed a bit
and finally allow
your mind to relax
and your body to rest—
will you still feel
a little depressed?

Of course you will feel it
'cause wounds are still fresh
and you'll still be feeling
that pain in your chest,
but an hour's an hour
and you'll make it through;

each hour gets easier—
I promise, it's true.

Will it matter tomorrow
when you wake up and rise
and your thoughts start to buzz
as you open your eyes,
and you think back to yesterday
slightly dismayed,
will it stop you from getting
along with your day?

Well it might, and that's fine—
that's what healing is for;
just know you're already
more healed than before,
for the worst—it has passed,
though you still have some pain,
keep in mind that most flowers
bloom after the rain.

Will it matter next week
when it's Monday again,
and you open your eyes,
and lift up your chin,
and you walk out the door
feeling newly refined—
will it really be worth
taking space in your mind?

Well a week's a short time
made of just seven days,

where resetting yourself
can be done several ways,
and though hurt lingers on
in the back of your mind,
you can start to look forward
instead of behind.

Will it matter next month
or the next or the next?
In three months will you feel
the same kind of effects
as you move on and up
with the life that you've made
from the shambles of things
because you weren't afraid
to start building again
from what was to what is?
No, you'll see your success
was all yours, never his.

This healing takes time
but you'll make it, I swear,
even if things right now
don't feel at all fair,
'cause with time you'll discover
the world is all yours—
once you can accept that,
in happiness pours.

An Obstacle Course

I now know in life
we're meant to go through
a large sum of hardships
so we know we grew
at times where we thought
hope was gone, all was lost,
when in fact hope was brewing;
it just had a cost.

This cost is a cost
that we know all too well,
it's the kind that occurs
when we stoop low and sell
ourselves short for the ones
who aren't worth just one cent,
yet who take a large toll
and require time spent.

They take up our headspace
and linger with angst
and as time goes along
they rise in our ranks
so much so we believe
they're important to us,
for they stay long enough
and they build up our trust
as our hearts run ahead
of our heads far behind
and we run at this feeling

as though we are blind,
for they've fooled us to think
we aren't stupid this time—
we think we have won
and soared to our prime.

Then reality hits
and we're pulled back to earth
where we struggle to figure out
what we are worth
after someone who showed us
how good we once were
left without saying why—
what bad luck to incur.

But bad luck is merely
an obstacle course—
it's random and tough
but it tests your sheer force
so that when the time comes
and the finish line's near
you will race to the end
without doubt or fear,
'cause you'll know what you're worth—
you'll be built by your costs,
knowing all that you found
came from all that you lost.

Regret

We all have regrets,
they're what we grow from;
some change us for better,
some make us turn numb,
but regret is a word
that alone stands quite strong,
for it blatantly says:
"I know I've done wrong."

As humans, we struggle
to own our mistakes,
for acknowledging flaws
in ourselves really takes
a large sum of dignity—
something we keep
locked away in a place
that is untouched and deep;
so when we say "regret"
we tap into that place
and we own up to feeling
a bit of disgrace
about something we did
that hurt someone bad,
or about certain people
we wish we still had,
or about giving someone
what they didn't deserve—
those are kinds of regrets
that strike right on the nerve,

for regrets are mistakes
that we feel deep inside;
they are cringey and painful
but sit and reside
in our minds as moments
we wish we could redo,
as we look back in time
with perspectives anew,
and we wonder what caused us
to do what we did,
but in time we realize
we can't simply get rid
of the things we don't like
that are already done—
though we wish that we could,
chances of that are none.

So instead we lay groundwork,
preventatively,
to ward off any chance
of repeating, you see.

We build mindsets from frameworks
we base in regret,
which propel us all forward
once we have reset
and resigned from the job
of rejecting the past,
and instead turn to questions
we wished we had asked,
or time we wish we'd spent,
or love we wish we'd shared,

or tasks we wish we'd done
even though we were scared.

As we bear our regrets
we come face-to-face
with the worst we have done,
but what we must embrace
is that he who can't learn
from his biggest mistakes
will regret it with every
step that he takes.

Outrunning the Storm

We are told that in life
we must weather the storms
because storms create chaos
and chaos transforms
all of us to new beings—
new souls who adapt
to life's plentiful curveballs
without feeling trapped.

We grow with intent
to prepare for the storms—
bringing jackets, umbrellas
and such is the norm.

So we sit and we wait—
umbrellas in hand—
with belief we're prepared
to sit here and withstand
the conditions to come—
stronger winds, darker clouds,
facing lightning and thunder
and storm-fleeing crowds—
all the things storms can bring:
we're prepared for the worst
but what we're not prepared for
is when clouds disperse—

when the sun comes back out,
and the storm drifts away—

we sit stuck in fear
for the rest of the day,
for we're taught of these storms
and how long they can last,
but we're often not taught
of what comes when they pass.

So we miss out on puddles
to splash and dance through;
we miss out on how rain
makes the world feel brand new;
we forget that most storms
aren't enduring, but brief
and that after each storm
there is post-storm relief.

It's too often this happens—
we harp on the doom,
we anticipate problems
and let them consume
all the sunlight we have
in our lives day to day—
we waste most of our sunlight
awaiting the gray.

And I say what a waste—
what a waste of the sun.
We will always face storms,
some we'll never outrun.

But we *can* step outside
on a day that is bright

without thinking of all
the thunder in sight
and sit back and enjoy
life that should be the norm—
life that isn't about
just awaiting the storm,
but instead it's about
all the days in between,
where the sky's extra blue
and the grass is real green
and no jackets are worn,
no umbrellas in hand,
where there's only the sun
and a day left unplanned.

These are days that we need
more than most of us know;
this is something I wished
that I learned long ago.

Our Own Pace

All perfection is fake—
that's something we know,
but the thing we forget
is we weren't made to go
to great lengths to change people
to be what we choose,
because all of us differ
in our visions and views
and these views, they're formed
from the places we've been:
where our past has led us;
where we chose to begin.

And for all, these diverge
so we're all made unique:
from the stories we tell
to attention we seek,
from the way we find joy
to the way we build trust,
from the way we find pride
to the way we adjust
when we meet someone who
isn't what we'd expect,
and we start to find things
we think we can perfect
over time, subtly,
so they'd never know
we're trying to change them,
but ever so slow.

We do this differently,
but do it no less;
if you think that you haven't,
it's time to confess.

We're all guilty of trying
to change what we can't,
and this effort turns into
a wish without grant,
for we only will change
where we see change is fit,
'cause we're stuck in our ways
more than we can admit.

So all you might do
to transform and amend
certain things people buy
or events they attend,
I'll tell you: just stop.
You'll simply just fail.
It won't matter your methods—
you'll never prevail
because we're all fixed
in ways we won't change,
no matter how different,
no matter how strange
we may be to some people
who don't get our ways—
who see all of our flaws
as a way to appraise
who we are as a person:
what we're valued at,

and what we'd be worth
if we just changed "all that."

So I say: never change
and don't change someone else;
they are who they are,
let them be their own self,
'cause it isn't your job
and isn't your place;
we all change when we need
at our very own pace.

The Best Is Yet To Come

When good things fall apart
we see only the broken;
we don't often see doors
that may have been opened,
for the end of most things
means new things will begin,
but in order to move
and start over again,
we must know that bad times
are not bad at their core,
'cause they give us a chance
to evolve even more,
and we need to evolve—
we'd be stagnant if not;
take a moment to think
of the things you've been taught
by the worst of life's lessons
in difficult ways—
sure they caused you some pain
and some short-term delays,
but they took something from you
that didn't belong—
though you might not agree
you must still remain strong
'cause if something's not right
then good things can't ensue—
so fate takes certain things
just to benefit you.

This occurs over time—
things will come and they'll go—
but with each door that's shut
you'll undoubtedly know
it was all for the best,
for the best's yet to come;
'til then you're working
on the you you'll become.

You'll see down the road
when you've opened new doors
that you're much better off
than you once were before,
and I hope you will learn
that bad times matter most—
they toughen you up
but allow you to boast
of the story that brought you
to this very day
because life worked out
in its strange, twisted way.

So when things don't go right,
don't get knocked off your feet
'cause the future you've got
will not stand for defeat,
and remember all endings
are beginnings as well;
these beginnings make life
the best story to tell.

Worth

To be shown that you're worth
more than you'd thought
is a gift that I think
people don't get a lot
'cause we all get stuck
when we're left all alone—
it's a sadness we feel
in each muscle and bone
as we slowly but surely
reduce what we are
despite all work we've put
into getting this far.

They say, "Love yourself.
You don't need to be told
of the great that you are
and the beauty you hold."

But I say that is hard
in ways they don't know,
for we learn from the people
who come and who go,
and when all that you know
are the ones who've gone—
who've come in so charming
but left as a con—
it's hard to believe
that you're worth more than that,

so instead of just standing,
we tend to fall flat.

And it's here we all need
someone brave and strong-willed
who can stand us up straight
and help us to rebuild.

And this is the gift
that I mentioned above—
it's the dear priceless gift
of re-learning self-love.

It comes not with a bow
but a feeling inside;
you will feel as it grows—
it can't be set aside;
but the person who gives this,
they're special indeed
for to show someone more
than attention and greed
seems so simple. It does.
And it is, to be real;
though the difference is small,
it lets someone else feel:
feel like someone again,
fill with comfort and trust—
it's a big change at first
but you'll quickly adjust,
for once you can love
what you've learned to suppress

you will never again
try to settle for less.

Her

Leaving her's the mistake
that he makes when he's young
but regrets when he's older and aged,
'cause once he's done
being fooled by fake beauty
he'll realize that hers wasn't staged.

He'll recognize humor
is wholly important—
that laughter should happen each day,
then he'll remember
her wonderful laugh
as something he'd like to replay.

He'll find that intelligence
has a high value;
it's something that's not just for show,
then he'll think about her—
all the things she's accomplished,
and what she once taught him to know.

He'll discover opinions
are meant to be different,
though everyone has rights to theirs,
then he'll summon to mind
that she never questioned
the thoughts and beliefs he had shared.

He'll learn authenticity
comes from within,
not from what you're told you should be,
but then he'll recall
how she forged her path
without caring what others might see.

He'll see independence
is something that's grown
by women whose strengths don't subside,
then he'll see her
making way for the world
without him right there by her side.

She's the kind of a woman
that he takes for granted;
one he thinks he'll find everywhere—
then many years later
when he is still looking,
he'll realize that she was so rare.

He'll see what he needs
is the natural, the stable—
a woman whose beauty is pure,
then he'll sit, looking back
wishing just to rewind—
who'd've thought all along

it was her.

Done

Today I am done
jumping oceans for people
who wouldn't jump puddles for me;
today I am through
wasting time on those people
who like me but don't want to be
any kind of involved
with the things that I do
or the life that I'm choosing to live;
today I will stop
choosing people who take
everything, but don't ever give.

Today I am done
making things all too easy
for people who make things too hard;
today I am through
letting walls down for people—
from now on I'll always keep guard
of what makes me open
and vulnerable
to those who know what to say
to get me to do
what they want me to do,
just to have them walk away.

Today I'm done giving
second chances to those
who were hardly worth giving a first;

today I am through
defending the people
who've made me feel worse at my worst,
for if someone can see
I've been through tough times
and chooses to put me through more
then I will stand up
for the sake of myself
and walk out of their very front door.

Today I am done
wondering if it's me
because as time has told, that's not true,
yes, today I am through
letting those who have failed me
reduce me to "someone they knew,"
for I'd hope I am someone
they wouldn't forget
due to the time I put in
to satisfy them
on their quaint little thrones
just to have them get under my skin.

Today I'm done guessing.
Today I'm done waiting,
done playing, done being tossed out,
done wasting my time,
done putting in effort,
done being weighed down by this doubt.

Yes today is the day
where I put my foot down.

You want sympathy here? There is none.
'Cause from now on I'll tolerate
 no more of this:

Today is the day I am done.

PART II:

THE COOKING

———

CHAPTER 4

STIRRING IN SAVORY

Throw It Out

Hate is a word
we use with great force;
it occurs when we meet
what we can't endorse—
be it lying, betrayal,
or differing views;
it's full of emotion
and hard to diffuse,
but I think in this world
when you have lots of hate
you put onto your shoulders
the heaviest weight,
for to hate is a way
to cultivate rage,
and it burdens you greatly
each year that you age.

As you carry this weight
it can slow you right down,
dragging you underwater
so you fear you might drown
in this hate that you feel
that consumes how you live
and affects the opinions
and efforts you give
to the rest of your life—
your family and friends,
who you treat differently
'cause you can't make amends

with the thoughts in your head
and the hate that you feel;
you obsess over it
and allow it to steal
your sanity, happiness,
strength, drive and trust,
so you must let it go,
no but's here, you must!

This means taking the high road—
it's not often used,
for when people see it
they're fairly confused
because here on the high road
hate's tossed to the side,
and what stands in its place
is a strong sense of pride
and in time, this pride wins;
yes it trumps all the hate—
it creates conversations
and opens the gate
for new dialogues, talks,
new debates and remarks;
it creates understanding
where once, it was stark.

The high road's the place
where our hate changes face;
it's where something of harm
turns to something of grace,
and in time staying high's
how we climb to great heights,

as opposed to diminishing
in our own fights.

Real

To be real in a world
that's pure make-believe
is a thing that so few
have the will to achieve,
for in life there are times
when it pays to be fake,
but in truth that is what
causes people to break,
for to feel stuck within
a strange place that's not you
simply wears you away
and wears you right through,
for our skin is our skin
and it's no one's but ours,
and to own it shows pride
through the bruises and scars
and perhaps the one way
to feel true in our skin
is to find those rare people
who have beauty within—
for to find someone real
who sees beauty in you
is a beautiful thing
that allows you to do
all the things that you love
and the things that you need
with a hand on your back
pushing you to succeed.

But the people like that
don't just wait from afar;
they arrive when you find
who you know that you are,
for as long as you're lost
in a world that's pretend
you won't find the person
who'll be your best friend.

And I speak from the heart
when I say for a fact
that when you know yourself
you'll always attract
the best things in life,
be it passion or trust,
that will make you feel real
in the ways I've discussed,
and I don't think I've known
any person to be
as incredibly, wonderfully
wild as me
except for the person
who knows me the best—
who is nothing but real,
and for that I am blessed,
'cause this best friend, she gave me
a reason to be
someone bold, unafraid,
with a soul that is free,
not confined by the feeling
of "staying in line"—

she taught me to own me
and all things that are mine.

Dots

If you judge by your ear
and your narrowed-down eyes
you won't see what you wanted to see;
think about the short phrase,
"Don't judge books by their cover,"
then sit and listen to me:

To grasp those six words
go and look at a map;
place your finger on somewhere you like;
trace your finger across
the one trail you would take
if you went through that country by bike.

From your finger-length view
you can see the big scheme:
where the cities aren't cities but dots,
and the two-inch-wide space
appears manageable,
and you like it much more than you thought.

Now I've been here before—
I know just how it goes,
you sit there and pore over the facts
about tourist attractions
and places to sleep—
about how people there tend to act.

At this point I suggest
that you go book a flight
and you visit the place you picked out,
and then fly to the midst
of a foreigner's land
and start biking through your traced route.

I'm not sure where you'd be—
where your finger touched down—
but I know you'd be simply in awe
at the difference between
just one dot on a map
and a place full of new land and laws,
and the people and voices,
and languages spoken
that swirl all around in your head;
you may find that this feeling's
more powerful than
anything that you'd seen, heard, or read.
'Cause you see, here's the problem
with pointing at maps:
they put distance where distance won't do,
because touching a place
versus feeling a place
is a difference that changes your view.

And I parallel maps
with the way that we judge
not because maps are so paramount,
but because they hold more
things and places combined
than the places that we could just count.

Maps are worlds full of words
holding words full of worlds
yet they never come close to complete,
but the more you explore
then the closer you get
to a view that is whole and unique.

And for every feature
that you can observe
there's a million more to go find,
which is why you can't judge
by the blink of one eye—
that's precisely how life was designed.

To Those With Egos

Have you ever met someone
who oozes conceit?
Who expects you to love them
and drop at their feet,
'cause they're simply that great
but they already know,
so they do everything
in their power to show
that they've done it all right
and have worked it all out?
Yes, these egos, they grow
'til it's all they're about
because egos get big
when accomplishments rise—
some heads can inflate
to ten times their own size
all because they are fooled
to think money and skill—
how well they throw balls
or how much they can bill—
makes them better than others
in all other ways,
when in fact, you're not better
'cause you got a raise!

Yet some with success
sit without any noise,
without flexing or spending
on cars and new toys,

they're just there and they're proud
but they do not need proof—
they don't go around screaming
success from the roof,
'cause they're humble: a word
some forget over time
as they chase and they push
others down as they climb
to the top of the world
where the money pours in:
they're in it for themselves;
they're in it to win.

And I feel for these people:
they chase and they chase
passing all of life's fun
at a rapid-speed pace,
and when they're finally done
they realize they *should* care,
for they reach the tip-top
and it's lonely up there.

It's lonely when image
is all that you've got,
and all you can show
are the things that you've bought,
for material goods
show the wealth you've amassed
but the pleasure they bring
disappears pretty fast,
which is why greedy people
are never content,

'cause their lives, they revolve
around every last cent
and instead of considering
anyone else
they remain solely focused
on only themselves.

They forget other people
make life worth the ride
and that others, they ground us
and shield us from pride—
pride that blinds us from life,
pride that blocks others out,
pride that makes us forget
what our lives are about.

Other people remind us
and keep us aware
that it pays to work hard,
but it pays more to care.

And so here's a reminder
that's close to my heart:
it can't hurt to be humble;
you just have to start.

Privilege

Most of us can't accept
that we're not always right;
we'll deny it until
our words lead to a fight:
one that could've been stopped
if we'd just paused to see
that we'd be more aligned
if we'd simply agree
that we're all human beings,
but not without flaws—
we stand by our beliefs
but don't stand by our laws
that we made to make sure
we all live the same way—
the pure irony there
is enough to convey
that we're quite inconsistent
in what we believe,
though we make some exceptions
so we can perceive
daily life as we like
so it works to our gain,
and we like it this way
so we always remain
all closed off to the rest
who may disrupt our bliss:
we're alike in the way
that we're often amiss
in the way we seek peace,

yes, we've got it all wrong:
we don't see that our flaw
is that we're too headstrong.

We're unwilling to change
in the wake of the worst,
'cause we're always too willing
to put ourselves first.

So you see what I mean:
we are selfish, that's it;
it's our one common flaw
that you have to admit
binds us closer than ever
yet tears us apart
so much so that we feel
we can't try to restart.

So we stay in this place
where we're all always right.
And we stay here all day.
And we stay here all night.
And we hold down our ground,
and we do not give in,
though it's useless to try
and believe we will win.

For if we cannot shift
and reset our minds,
then we still will proceed
to be senseless and blind
to what needs to be changed

and what needs to be done;
if we stay narrow-minded
we'll be at square one
'til we compromise thought
and we look at the "why,"
and realize we're one
living under one sky—
we breathe in the same air,
and we walk the same ground,
and we've grown as a species
from what we have found
to be true in this world
be it science or peace,
and I think that it's time
that we finally release
the belief that we're right
in a world that is wrong;

it's in realizing weakness
that we become strong.

Trapped

Nowadays we are trapped
by the standards we set
for each other's success,
cause we've come to forget
that success comes from passion
and loving your work,
whether you are a doctor,
a teacher, a clerk—
when it comes to your job
it should be up to you,
but society's taught us
to only pursue
jobs that make us most rich
where we prosper with ease
in the eyes of the world
and the profit it sees,
but in turn we've lost sight
of success in true form
as we've tossed off our callings
and come to conform
to the status-ranked chain
where we're cogs in a wheel
trying hard to rise up
to achieve the best deal.

We've come to a point
where we measure ourselves
and what we've become
against everyone else,

'cause success as a word
has been taken apart
by a world that can't value
all skill and all art
with a level perception
of what they provide
to a world that's gone blind
to what brings us alive.

We accept this as truth
'til we choose that it's not,
and we take back success
and the dreams that we'd sought
and we make them our own
and pave way for the rest
who've got dreams that've been
overlooked or suppressed.

With power in numbers
we can all redefine
the word of success
and the way we align
with the standards we set
in which we forgot
that we're meant for much more
than we had once thought.

Anxious

There are times when our thoughts
become jumbled inside,
when there's simply no place
for our "calm" to reside;
when we can't find the quiet
within our own head
and our sanity's hanging
by merely a thread,
and ideas bounce around,
but no words are kept straight
and all sides of our brain
are in heated debate
about what we should do
or what we should think next—
yes, the great human mind
is obscenely complex
with its thousands of thoughts
flying through at great speeds
with ambitions to satisfy
all of our needs
and get everything done
so that we can calm down,
though we feel in our heads
that we maybe might drown
in these thoughts that take up
all the space in our brain
in a way that sometimes
we cannot contain…

So we lose it a bit.
Not just you—we all do.
'Cause anxiety's real,
and a real hassle too.

We've been programmed to have
hyperactive, smart minds
so that we can grow up
to reach goals of all kinds.
And that's fine, goals are good.
We work towards them each day,
but the side effects come
in a number of ways:

we're overwhelmed, tired,
distressed and uptight,
spending days in our heads,
staying up late at night;
we're consumed with the need
to be perfect: just right,
so as we keep going
we start to lose sight
of what matters to us
and what matters right now—
the one problem is
that we rarely allow
ourselves any spare moment
to get our thoughts out—
so we keep them up there
as they clang and they shout
and make deafening noise
'til we set them all free—

let them out in the open
so that we can see
that we aren't all okay
but that *that* is okay,
and more people, they realize this
every new day.

'Cause our intricate minds
are a stunning, strange place
that are easily hid
by a false smiling face;
and we all know this face—
it allows us to hide
the times when our thoughts
become jumbled inside.

So a fact you should keep
in your mind as you go
is that people feel more
than you might ever know,
and if you are someone
who feels more than we see,
know that you are allowed
to set certain thoughts free.

Value

We seek validation
in all kinds of forms
not because we enjoy it,
but 'cause it's the norm—
'cause we've been convinced
that we must be assured
that we're doing okay
and that we have secured
a place in this world
that will make us stand out;
we seek others' approval
as way to gain clout,
and we're always so eager
to please others' tastes
that some parts of ourselves
become slowly erased.

So we've built up a world
that can't stand on its own
because people can't find
validation alone.

And when we're alone
with our mind and our thoughts
without others opinions
to tie us in knots,
we are mean to ourselves;
we aren't nice, we aren't kind
for the whole world's opinion

has been intertwined
in the way that we feel
about things that we do,
so much so that we can't
seem to find our own views
amongst all the assumptions,
and stereotypes,
all the attitudes, judgments,
impressions and gripes
people always will have
about us and the rest—
this is something that's true,
though it's tough to digest.

So I've realized that there's
a solution to this:
it's to realize that ignorance
really is bliss.

It's to know you can't please
every soul on this earth,
but that no one's opinion
reduces your worth.

It's to think to yourself:
"Wow, I am pretty great,"
as opposed to degrading
each one of your traits,
'cause in fact you are great,
despite what you might think,
and I think what's important
is finding the link

between you and the people
who value your views—
finding people who *value*
not validate you.

Starting Out

If you're thinking out loud
and you've got a good thought,
you should put it in motion
if you like it a lot
because so many thoughts
are simply passed by
by ingenious people
who don't want to try
to achieve bigger things
and step out of their zone
into things that are new,
and are often unknown.

But it's people like this
who as one halt our pace
in advancing our world
as the great human race—
and I see why they stop,
there's no promise to win,
yet if they want a chance
they must simply begin.

Because every big thing
starts as something that's small,
for it takes just one brick
to begin a brick wall,
but I think that the fear
of the small starting out
is a fear that creates

quite a strong sense of doubt,
and with doubt in our minds
we are set up to lose
for we've got what we need
and we've got the right views,
but the one simple thing
that we're missing a lot
is the reason just why
we believe in our thought,
for from faith we gain strength
and the will to persist
into making our thoughts
come to life and exist.

And once work follows faith
little things start to grow,
and as time runs along
all that hard work will show,
and if others can see
just how hard we have tried,
well then I do believe
we've got luck on our side,
for the more that we work
the more luck we attain,
and the less fear we have
the more triumph we gain.

Smartest Person in The Room

I don't think the word intelligence
can really be described
by how we count our numbers
or do work that we're assigned;
I think it's so much more than that—
much more than we express these days,
I think intelligence is quite
the underestimated phrase,
'cause to me it means awareness—
it's how to listen, when to smile;
it's how to take someone's emotions
and give them back something worthwhile.

It's having empathy at times—
obtaining other points of views;
it's knowing people's feelings toward you
hinge on certain words you choose.

It's reading rooms and shutting up
when you've got nothing good to say;
it's finding balance in your life—
how much you work, how much you play.

I think intelligence is silence
in moments when you want to talk;
it's knowing when you need to listen
and how to be somebody's rock.

I think it's righting people's wrongs
but also letting people learn,
it's sitting back but standing up enough
to voice a real concern.

It's telling anger from frustration,
discerning doubt from simple fear;
it's knowing when you're being played
and when intentions are sincere.

I think intelligence is common sense—
it's learned from what you do,
'cause you can sit in class for years
and still come out without a clue;
yes, being smart requires growing up
and truly working hard,
it means achieving the maturity
to always first regard
the way that other people act:
how they behave, how they respond,
because becoming "people smart"
requires thought that goes beyond
the facts you'll learn inside your school,
it's based on something much more real—
it's how you interact with everyone
and how you make them feel.

It's our humanity that binds us;
it's the connection that we build
and as you learn this going forward
you'll become more highly skilled,
for if you learn to simply listen

and not to talk and just assume,
I guarantee you'll always be
the smartest person in the room.

I've Been Thinking

I think getting to know
the way someone thinks
is a process that takes
ample time but then syncs
your two brains together
so that you can see
each other's perspectives—
how they came to be,
'cause we arrive in this world
like a ball made of clay
that is kneaded and rolled up
and shaped in a way
that is constantly changing
but cast from a mold
that we can't ever change
even as we grow old,
for although we try hard
to adapt and reshape,
where we come from is something
that we can't escape,
for it's what we are made of
at our very core,
but it doesn't determine
what we have in store.

Though some think that it does,
stuck in bubbles, they live
without hope to grow more
and unwilling to give

into whimsical life
and the wonders it holds,
all because they're too stuck
in their unchanging molds.

See, I know how they think.
I've been stuck where they are.
And I realized that mindset
won't get you too far.

So I've come to accept
that to forge a new mold,
we must branch out to things
that aren't always controlled
and grow knowledge with effort
that stems from a drive
to know more about others
and how they survive
in their day to day tasks
and the passions they choose;
how they grow from resistance
or heal from a bruise,
for from others we learn
that to learn is to be
open-minded to people
who live and who see
the world different from you
but who show you that thought
is most valuable when
it is shared and well taught.

To Put It Simply

We all believe
we're very different,
when we're really quite the same,
we go through life
in worlds divided
and it's really quite a shame
'cause in this world
we're not alone,
though many people think they are;
the way we see things
disconnects us
so we feel we're very far
from other cultures,
other people,
other ways and walks of life;
we stay in line
and mind our business
without desire to unite,
and so our hunger
to learn more
about our world begins to flee;
I wish we knew
that we've all got
much more in common than we see:

We live to work,
we all get tired,
more sleep is always in demand;

we like to know what's coming next,
but many things arrive unplanned.

All books have words,
all words have sounds,
all humans have the right to read;
all countries give us different rights,
but some don't give the ones we need.

Wood comes from trees,
trees make the woods,
we breathe because we have the trees;
a good deep breath can calm you down,
sometimes it's hard to be at ease.

Buildings have walls
to hold them up
but not all doors can keep things out—
sometimes we don't let people in,
some people we can live without.

Our metal rusts,
our seams get torn,
things fall apart when they get old;
our secrets lose their right to secrecy
as soon as they get told.

We weaponize
our many words
but do not realize how they harm;
we all have done some harmful things,
but every person has a charm.

We like to think
we know it all
but write reminders we forget;
we like to say we've beat our fears
even when we haven't yet.

The world is big,
the earth is small,
perspective puts you into place;
cheetahs run faster than us humans,
but many humans love to race.

You might be here,
I might be there,
but distance doesn't mean we're far;
we're contradictory in nature,
but that is just how humans are,
'cause we're complex
but life is simple—
we live in paradox each day,
and consequently
we're connected
in a million different ways.

CHAPTER 5

CREATING NEW RECIPES

———

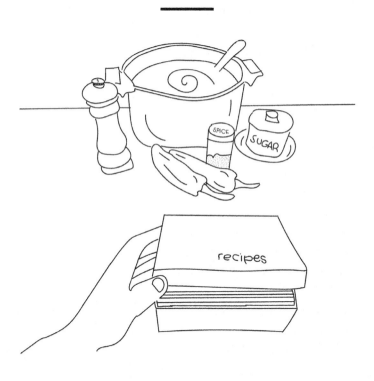

Happiness Is

I believe the best thing
that somebody can say—
doesn't matter the time
or the place or the day—
is that you look happy:
not much, I know,
but to change your demeanor
so much that it shows
and shines brightly to others
who can't help but see
is a stunning achievement,
you have to agree.

For from inside to out
you are glowing a lot,
and I think that this change
is a change that we ought
to applaud people for—
boost them up, give them praise,
tell them how good they look
in the friendliest ways,
because people work hard
to be happy, you see—
they work to make life
a place they can be
always striving toward good
but still getting good back,
yet still looking to better
the traits that they lack.

The best happy is balance
of change and the same—
it's a state of diminishing
envy and shame
and embracing life's good
in all ways you know how,
because happiness means
that you're living *right now.*

So I think to be happy
in ways people see
means you're doing it right;
you are living life free
of the stress of the past
and the future to come;
you aren't stuck stiffly under
society's thumb.

Instead you accept
that you're calm and content
with the places you're going
and the places you've went,
so you live in the present:
this moment right here,
with a mind that is open
and a vision that's clear,
and you radiate light
with the joy that you show—
it's a wonderful thing
to see someone else glow.

Thankful

I'm thankful for my life—
I'm thankful just to be alive,
I'm thankful for the fights I've fought
that also taught me to survive.

I'm thankful for the ones who love me
and for how they've made me I feel,
I'm thankful for the parts of life
that seem too wondrous to be real.

I'm thankful for the helping hands
who led me right where I should be,
I'm thankful for what I've been taught
and for what life has given me.

Though there's one thing I wish I had—
one thing I would be thankful for,
but it's impossible to have,
and of that fact I'm very sure.

I'll still tell you what I wish:
I wish somehow there was a way
to live more life inside our lives
with extra hours in the day.

What would you do with extra hours?
Would you sit down and write a book?
Would you go run a marathon?
Or would you teach yourself to cook?

I know that one thing I would do
is spend more time of mine outside,
for with more hours in the day
we'd have more sunshine in our lives.

Another thing that I would do
is take more time to find myself,
whether that's swimming in the sea
or taking new books off the shelf.

And with this time that I would have
I'd meet more people, see more sights;
I'd have more smiles, laughs, and giggles,
more happy days at higher heights.

These days we don't have much free time,
but we could use a little more
to take some moments to ourselves
to realize what we're thankful for.

So though the clock is always ticking,
know that every second counts,
for in small seconds we can change the world
in very big amounts.

All Ya Gotta Do

When you give it your all
and give it your best,
you should know that you've passed
most of life's biggest tests,
for to know that you've tried
and done all you can do
is a striking achievement
that speaks about you
and the drive that you have—
the ambition you've got
to advance in the world
and shoot your own shot,
'cause most people aren't like that—
they lack the true grit
to rise up to a challenge
and truly commit
to a path that's demanding
but worth what it takes
to invest and persist
at the highest of stakes
'cause it takes perseverance
that's constant, sustained,
and it takes many habits
that must be maintained
despite any failure
that may come about—
when you give it your all
there's no easy way out.

'Cause the one truest thing
in all things I've learned
is that all real success
is success that is earned.

So you must know in life
that your will to push on
and your drive to achieve
will lead you upon
the success you should want
and the things you deserve,
for though we can't account
for life's unforeseen curves,
we can keep in our minds
that we get what we give,
and that all things are based
on the ways that we live.

So my friend, keep on going—
if life pushes, you pull;
everything you give now
you will get back in full.

Thank You, Mom

Without my mom I wouldn't see
the different shades of ocean blue:
how they change in different eyes
depending on your point of view,
and many blues are beautiful
but not all blues can match to me,
'cause I'm my own bright shade of blue
that only special eyes can see.

Without my mom I wouldn't trust
the sea is full of many fish
who may not all be meant for me
regardless of how much I wish,
but for the ones that swim away
she taught me how to stay afloat,
and how to keep wind in my sails
just like a giant sailing boat.

Without my mom I wouldn't think
to check the tides before I wade,
and if I find I'm in too deep
I shouldn't ever be afraid,
because the ocean is forgiving,
and I'm marvelously strong,
and if I keep on swimming upwards
then it cannot do me wrong.

Without my mom I wouldn't know
that life is simply like a beach—

it stretches on for many miles,
some just too far for me to reach.

But don't you worry, I know now
that leaving footprints in the sand
is more important in my life
than staying static where I stand,
for though they wash away in time
they tracked the trail that led me here,
and I belong right where I am
no matter what may disappear,
for there is wonder in the ocean
that works beyond the human eye
that makes each moment beautiful
and puts the blue into the sky.

So thank you Mom, for showing me
that life may pass by day by day,
but how it's measured is in moments
that simply take my breath away.

The Power of One

A single word can mend a cut,
a tighter hug can fix an ache,
a kiss can be your biggest fear,
or be the leap you need to take.

A single wave can make you smile,
the slightest touch can soothe your soul,
the love you find may break you down,
but one day it will make you whole.

A single moment can be scary,
but looking back it's nothing bad;
the time you want to fly will fly,
and one day that might make you sad.

A single action is a mirror
that instantly reflects on you,
and when you get back what you give,
you'll understand yourself anew.

A single person with a brain
who's got a heart as big to match
is worth a lot more than the people
who stay a little, then detach.

A single step in one direction
may take you down a path that's wrong,
but one day after you have straightened out
you'll be where you belong.

A single flaw can be a struggle
or a way to open doors,
but you'll get nowhere in your life
if you don't claim what's really yours.

A single choice to be yourself
amongst a crowd with narrow eyes
is something that you can't regret—
it's something that will make you wise.

But most importantly, I think,
the single thing that you must know
is that it's not what you can talk about,
but only what you show,
because there's power in the small:
the little acts that make our days—
the things we always take for granted
and neglect in many ways.

We often all forget small things
give us our courage and our strength
to put in lots of extra efforts
and to go the extra lengths
to be the people that we want—
the ones we always sought to be;
"It's the little things," they say,
something to which I must agree.

So keep in mind that just one thought
can be the only hope you need,
for any plant that's ever grown
has always started with a seed.

Stitched

Our lives are like quilts:
they're patched up and sewn
with love we have found
and people we've known;
they're bursting with colors
and raggedy seams—
a lifetime of wonder
and long-deserved dreams.

These quilts are unique—
each one crafted with care;
they're perfect despite
the occasional tear,
but these tears are quite small
in the grand scheme of things—
amongst millions of patches
and miles of strings
that are woven together
from all that you've done—
here the yous you've grown through
are all tied into one!

Yes, one beautiful quilt—
your hard-earned work of art—
that you've crafted each day
from your very young start.

Our quilts grows as we grow;
with each day we add more

and as time goes along
we look back and adore
all the patches we've made
from the lives we have led,
all while knowing we still
have a whole life ahead.

But we don't know our best days
'til they've all but passed
at a rate that seemed slow
but now seems all too fast
because time's an illusion
that plays with our heads
as our life's sewn together
with memory threads
that stitch moments and feelings,
photos and dates,
our smiles and tears,
and impressions and traits,
into one stretch of time
that we carry somehow
from the day we were born
to this moment right now!

And these memory threads,
they are woven with care;
they connect every patch
and make each of us rare,
for they bind up our past
and they craft us to be
who we look in the mirror
and finally see,

'cause despite all our feats
and all roles we have played,
we are all just a sum
of the memories we've made.

So be proud of the quilt
you have made all these years
that is both full of joy
and a million fears;
it is beautifully you—
all your best quirks combined—
and the legacy one day
that you'll leave behind.

Half Full

One day, my mother shared with me
a piece of critical advice;
her words were quite astounding
and made me think about life twice.

It was a day when I was angry,
a little bitter towards the world,
so she turned to me and said,
"Now listen up my growing girl:
no life is perfect, that's a given,
but if you listen and obey
to these few tips I have for you
you might see things a different way.

First off, pretend the trees are castles;
pretend you live the life of kings,
and even when your kingdom falls,
pretend it's on a big upswing.

You must wake up to smell the roses
even if there's none to smell,
and if you ever have an argument,
you must make sure not to dwell.

Dear, search for pictures in the clouds
even when a storm is brewing,
and when the sun is shining on you,
smile no matter what you're doing.

Please sit and paint a little butterfly—
observe the flutter of its wings—
and when you have a little daughter,
please clear your day to hear her sing.

Look up above to see the stars
even if the night's real dark,
and when you meet a boy you really like,
look closely for that spark!

Make a list of things you love
and one for things you want to do,
and maybe when you've turned 100,
you'll have seen your whole list through.

But most of all, please understand
that your whole life, it will depend
on who you choose to make your enemy,
and who you choose to make your friend.

Just be aware of optimism
and all the power it can hold;
make sure you keep your spirits up
and as you come to getting old,
make sure that 1+1 is always two
and that two halves make a whole,
but your first task of every day
should be to pour your glass half full."

A Toast

Cheers to all of life's ditches
and all mountain tops;
cheers to all of the green lights
and all of the stops.

Cheers to all of the roadblocks
and all of roads;
cheers to carrying burdens
and lightening loads.

Cheers to falling down seven times,
getting up eight;
cheers to letting things happen
and going with fate.

Cheers to laughing to tears,
'til your sides nearly split;
cheers to proving your power
and finding your grit.

Cheers to leaning on shoulders
at times when you need;
cheers to working on teams
but still taking the lead.

Cheers to growing up slow
but not aging at heart;
cheers to finishing things
but beginning at start.

Cheers to going the distance,
prevailing with grace;
cheers to chasing your dreams
knowing it's not a race.

Cheers to having good friends
who love you just for you;
cheers to knowing you have people
you belong to.

Cheers to life that gives life,
cheers to every new day;
cheers to making mistakes,
cheers to paving your way.

Breathe

Take a breath. Just one breath.
Just breathe in and breathe out.
Feel the freshness of air in your soul,
and with this breath of air
take a moment to realize
what you can and cannot control.

'Cause as humans we strive
to seek every step
and make sure it happens as planned,
but when things start to change
and our worlds turn around,
we struggle with matters at hand.

We can't handle the things
that are out of our hands
that run wild, away from our grasp,
and in turn we lose structure—
what's kept us together—
like a necklace that loses its clasp.

And in times when we feel
that we're slightly unhinged
and begin to all go a bit mad,
I just wonder how people
find hope in the world
when there isn't a trace to be had.

I've realized that hope
is like money these days—
it's traded and taken and spent,
and if you put your own
in the wrong kinds of hands,
you'll be down to your very last cent.

But the thing about money
is that it is given—
we earn it from others who pay;
be it paychecks or charity,
money is given
because we all need it each day.

We don't think about hope
in this mindset at all,
but I think going forward, we should,
because realizing hope
is essential to life
would do all of us large sums of good.

So any you have—
any small shred of hope—
I encourage that you pass it on
for if we do not pass it
then it will diminish
and eventually it will be gone.

We want to believe
in the best at the worst,
but we never can do this alone;
we need others to give

any hope that they have
so we can have hope of our own.

So in times just like this,
take a breath. Just one breath.
Feel the air circulate through your veins,
and with this breath of air
take a moment to realize
that crisis brings everyone pains.

Take a moment to feel
just how full that you are
in a world that's so empty these days;
take that fullness you have
and go give some to someone
so they can have hope in new ways.

A Little Faith

If there's ever a day
when you're down and out
and unsure what's next—
hesitating from doubt—
'cause the world's got to you
in a new kind of way
making you question you
in this time of much say
when life's moving fast
but your mind's staying still
and you're keeping your wits
but you're losing your will
as the future looms large
and you stand feeling small...

Well, hold on for a second—
you're not seeing it all!

Ah yes, I see it now.
I can see it real clear.
One day you're gonna have
the most booming career!
All those years of hard work
and long nights of no sleep—
they will one day pay off,
and rewards you will reap.

You will light up the world
with your wonderful ways,

and meet so many people
who will all sing your praise.

So if you've got doubt
or an ounce of distress,
know that you've got in store
a great bout of success—
you might not believe it,
but just know that I do,
so if you need a booster,
you know who to turn to.

'Cause with so many smarts
and a heart full of gold
and ideas that are new
but a soul that is old,
I've no doubt that for you
things will ever be slow,
and I can't wait to see
all the places you'll go.

What I'd Give

What I'd give to go back
to a time where I thought
that to color in lines
was achieving a lot;
to a time where my mind
was at peace with most things,
back when I was beginning
to sprout my own wings
to soar into a life
with great grace and finesse,
with a crown on my head
in my fairytale dress
as my fears dropped away,
and my dreams became grand;
at age five, I stood proud
with my whole life planned.

It was simple back then—
details didn't exist,
any worries or stressors
were merely dismissed
at the blink of an eye
'cause the world, it was mine:
I had decades ahead
to begin to design
a life I would be proud
to grow into one day—
at that time it could go
really any which way

that I wanted it to,
so I set on my path:
I did all my readings
and studied my math;
I learned sentences, cursive,
wrote many reports,
and I tried my fair hand
at a number of sports,
I made friends, many friends,
and I lost a few too,
but I kept going on,
yes, I grew and I grew,
and I laughed a whole lot
but I learned even more;
though it wasn't 'til now
I learned what it was for—

it was for this, right now.
This one moment right here
when I get my diploma
and shed a few tears
as I realize how special
each moment has been—
how I came to be me,
how I came to begin
on a path that allowed me
to do the best things—
on a path where I spread out
my powerful wings
and I took off with strength,
and found some on the way—

this strength carried me here
to this so-special day.

It is not 'til right now
while I stand on this stage
looking out at the crowd
on this chapter's last page
that I realize how much
I would give to go back
to a day that was made
by an after-school snack:
a day where I smiled—
no cares in the world—
as a little and confident
five-year-old girl.

But I think of young me—
what she wanted to do;
all the dreams that she had,
all the colors she drew,
and I smile real wide
as I look to the crowd
'cause I know without doubt
I have made her so proud.

Things I've Learned

Take the chances you can,
don't live to compete;
all things happen in time,
every failure's a feat.

Your sole focus is you,
having patience is key;
helping hands get you through;
some things aren't meant to be.

Bad days stink when they're bad
but they make good days great;
having hope in your heart
is more healthy than hate.

One who cheats never wins,
laughing loud helps you heal;
many things seem so fake,
but look out for what's real.

To keep dwelling is bad
but emotions will stay;
you will feel many things
just don't push them away—
you may wish they weren't there
but time makes all things fade;
one day you'll come to love
all the feelings that stayed.

Better things are to come,
rainy days make things grow;
travel at your own pace—
it's okay if it's slow,
but to know where to quit
and to know where you stand
is like carving in stone
what you once set in sand.

Take on all that you can
without taking it all,
and seek alternate routes
when you're hitting a wall.

Do the things that you like,
don't waste time on the rest;
you don't need anything
that holds you from your best,
'cause to get from the world
what you want it to give,
you must not be afraid
to go out and just live.

ACKNOWLEDGEMENTS

I would first like to thank my mom, my dad, my two sisters, and my grandparents who have listened to me read so many poems over the years, always believing that I had it in me to write a book. They have been a never-ending source of love and encouragement, and I am forever grateful to all of them.

I would next like to acknowledge those who have given me endless support in the process of making this book come to life: Meghan Isaf, Samantha Mirchin, Brittany Loveless, Emma Tatum, Olivia Feldman, Allison Steiner, Aileen Reeves, Kristyn Mize, Maryellen Robinson, Sara Rowlands, Lauren Mazur, Gabrielle Ramirez, Paul Radovanovich, Katie Hooker, Joseph Alberico, Natalie Perlov, Elizabeth Ivanecky, Cady North, Haley Newlin, Ryan Conner, Katie Zinke, Alex Zinke, and Sandy Zinke.

I'd also like to gratefully acknowledge: The Stikeleather Families, The Feigh Family, The Ach Family, The Zinke Families, The Martin Family, The Beckwith Family, The Adler Family, The Wise Family, The Giordano Family, The Stephenson Family, The Berk Family, The Carr Family, Meghan Sobolewski, Karen Mascott, Todd Goodman, Christie Bailey,

Doug Gould, Brooke Gallaway, Sarah Ford, Chad Saulnier, Nancy Blackburn, Megan Mattaliano, and Lisa Villano.

Lastly, I'd like to say a special thank you to two friends of mine who love poetry just as much as I do and have always believed in me and my writing journey: Gabriella Etoniru and Michelle Wolf. Thank you for always reading my poems at all hours of the day and keeping me headed towards this dream of mine.

A final thank you to Eric Koester, who set me on this path of publishing. His writing program, the Creator Institute, has been life-changing for me, and has allowed me to grow so much as both a writer and a person.

Made in the USA
Middletown, DE
11 January 2021